Print information available on the last page

Rev. date: 01/07/2020

To order additional copies of this book, contact:
Xlibris
1-888-795-4274
www.Xlibris.com
Orders@Xlibris.com

Our Dads, Our Heroes

The Marine Corps War Memorial

The United States Flag Raising of Iwo Jima

FOREWORD

It is said that a picture is worth a thousand words. One World War II photo in particular has certainly surpassed that level of expectation: The iconic photo showing the raising of the flag during the battle of Iwo Jima.

The spirit of the moment was captured through the lens of photographer Joe Rosenthal; the image was immediately thrust into the national headlines. The Memorial was showcased on postage stamps, murals, magazine covers, and seen on what was to become the Marine Corps Memorial located in Arlington, Virginia, as well as replicas throughout the world.

Felix De Weldon created this eye-catching rendition of the photo through a piece of bronze which would forever immortalize the action of six brave Marines.

The Japanese attack on Pearl Harbor led the United States into the war throughout the Pacific, in an attempt to stop the Japanese from expanding their empire. It was the beginning of what would become a brutal and deadly battle that would encapsulate this historic battle.

This February, we recognize the 75th anniversary of Iwo Jima. Although the photo of the flag-raising became a well-recognized image –by many onlookers– worldwide, there has been some mystery concerning the individuals shown in the picture. Within a year of this photo's deemed release, it was brought about by Ira Hayes, one of the flag raisers, that the young man at the base of the flagpole, was indeed Harlon Block, and not Private Hanson. Seven decades later, in 2016, another Marine was announced to have been misidentified. Through a process known as photograph DNA, it was determined that John Bradley, although seen in many photos, was not actually in the coveted photo. Instead, this person was a Marine private named Charles Schultz. It should be noted that as of October 2019, the Marine Corps has announced another misidentified Marine, that of my dad: Rene Gagnon. The latest changes call out to PFC (Private First Class) Harold Keller. This announcement comes as a complete shock to our family, but we are relieved that the truth has come out and the marine who did raise the flag, was properly credited. Thank you, to all of you who read this book, for your understanding. The facts of this battle remain as poignant as ever.

Rene Gagnon Jr.

The United States Marine Corps War Memorial is a vast and vivid statue showcasing six brave young men who raised our American flag, claiming victory during the Battle of Iwo Jima during World War II. It weighs seven hundred tons and stands prominently in Arlington, Virginia, where so many Marines rest. You will see images of this statue in many different versions: photos, numerous books, other monuments throughout the country, magnets, T-shirts, hats…

This historical moment began with a famous photograph of the flag raising during the battle, captured by civilian photographer Joe Rosenthal. Within 48 hours Rosenthal's photo made front page in every major newspaper in America.

During the Second World War, Japan wanted to expand its Empire and gain as much control as possible. The Japanese had succeeded in taking over large parts of China and nearly all of the Pacific island groups. On December 7, 1941, they took the fight to the United States, when they attacked the US Navy base called Pearl Harbor in Hawaii. This was three years before Iwo Jima would be invaded. From the very beginning, Marines were fighting together to prevent more American boys from dying on the ships and on land. The civilians and families of the Marines and other servicemen thought that Japan might completely invade Hawaii to control it like it did all the other islands. Thanks to all the brave armed forces, the Japanese did not succeed. The Japanese commander even said after the attack that he feared "that we have awakened a sleeping giant," meaning that the Japanese would soon regret their decision to attack Pearl Harbor.

The attack on Pearl Harbor sounded the alarm that would bring the Americans into the Pacific battles of the "island-hopping" campaigns, specifically the strategically important island of Iwo Jima. Many of our young men would take the call to action and join the military to fight for freedom.

During the island-hopping campaign, numerous islands in the Pacific were invaded by the US Navy and reclaimed. One of these islands was Iwo Jima, a tiny spot on the map that would soon become known to the entire world.

Iwo Jima Island is a volcanic island in the Pacific, just over four miles long and two miles wide, which lies only about six hundred miles south of the Japanese city of Tokyo. Iwo Jima was used as an airbase by the Japanese during World War II, from which they attacked US bombers and other islands the Japanese wanted to take over. The United States needed to take the island to stop the Japanese from attacking their planes, and to have a place –closer to Japan– for the bombers to take off and land. Following months of bombing by Navy ships and American bomber planes, the US Marines landed on the small island on February 19, 1945.

Before the battle, all the Marines –most of which were only 18 or 19 years old– left their families and friends to go through boot camp training at Camp Pendleton, California and continued to Camp Tarawa on the island of Hawaii for further training. When they left Camp Tarawa on troop transports, they didn't know where they were going. Once they knew what they were in for, they wanted to go home to their mothers, their wives, and their friends, but they realized what had to be done. Sadly, many of the boys did not make it back home. Many of them were wounded (WIA) or killed in action (KIA) or went missing in action (MIA). For many of them, it was their first and only time in combat. The able-bodied survivors were sent back to Camp Tarawa for rest and later used as occupational forces in Japan after the surrender. Those who survived found their lives had changed forever with the gruesome thoughts of the images they observed during this bloody battle.

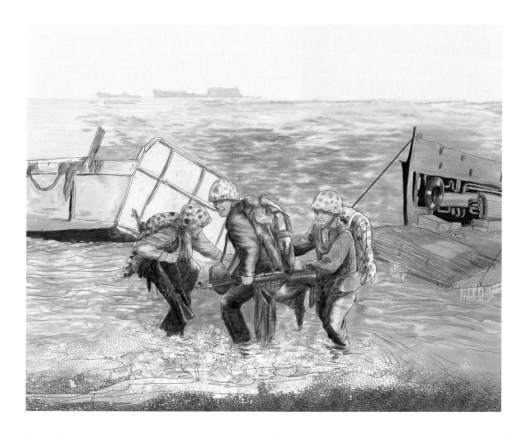

Some of the Marines who landed at Iwo Jima had also fought in earlier battles. Many Marines who were in the Fifth Marine Division at Iwo Jima had been paratroopers who landed by boat on other important islands like Guadalcanal ["Gwadal-canal"] and Bougainville ["Bowgun-vil"]. They then returned to the United States, were retrained and given new weapons, and went on to Sulphur Island (translation of Japanese 'Iwo Jima'). Even though when the Japanese on Iwo Jima had been conquered, the large island of Okinawa was still left to be secured. The Iwo Jima flag raising became a symbol of the victory which would soon come. A surrender that so many people around the world were hoping would bring their loved ones home safely.

Apart from their uniforms, the Marines had no protection, and immediately became concerned. They had to work diligently and speedily to move toward and up the mountain as their hidden enemy was ready to attack.

The main goal of the battle was to capture Mount Suribachi, a dormant volcano, as well as the two airfields on the island so that American pilots could attack the Japanese mainland in hopes that the Japanese would soon surrender and end the war.

As the navy landing ships dropped the young Marines on the larger-than-life island, thousands of feet hit the black sand that was so hard to walk or run in, and all looked up to the looming, dormant volcano Suribachi. The boys tried to find shelter from the enemy bullets, unable to see the Japanese who were hiding in caves. Our military, upon landing on the beach, found their tanks and themselves sinking into the sand that was hot from the underground lava.

On that first day of battle, seventy-five thousand troops took to the shores of the small island. They were told the battle would not take long. An officer told Mr. Wheeler it would be "a piece of cake." The first few days were horrific. In only three days, many of our American soldiers were caught in a crossfire while trying to remove the Japanese from Mount Suribachi, the highest part of the island.

Back in the States, propaganda depicted the Japanese as rat-like people with buckteeth and thick glasses. In reality they were highly disciplined, outstanding soldiers. The Japanese had been on Iwo Jima for months and they had transformed the island into a fortress. Over 15 miles of tunnels were dug, and more than 1,500 reinforced concrete strongholds dotted the island. In addition, there were numerous natural and man-made caves. Many Marines only saw living Japanese after the battle and felt like they had been fighting ghost during the 36 days of the campaign. The Japanese commander, Tadamichi Kuribayashi, had instructed his men to fight to the bitter end, and informed them that every man was to kill at least ten Americans before dying.

The Marines landed on the terraced black beaches in group called waves. The first few waves landed unopposed, and the Marines felt relieved. They did not yet realize that the Japanese had set a trap. When the beaches were full of men and equipment, the Japanese saw their chance. Heavy enemy fire raked the beaches and many Marines were wounded and killed.

On the fifth day, there was an eerie sense of calm. A commander then sent forty Marines to the top of the mountain. As they climbed up the slope, the Japanese were running around underground. The group reached the top safely and raised the Stars and Stripes, causing Marines all over the island and onboard ship to cheer and cry tears of relief and joy. The commander who had ordered the patrol wanted to keep the flag as a memento. The decision was made to hoist up another, larger flag. It was this flag that would go down in history as a symbol of victory and bravery. Rene Gagnon Sr. was sent to run the larger flag to the top of the mountain. However, the war was far from over.

Shortly after the battle, this picture was released. It shows the names and faces of the six flag raisers as they were initially identified. Seventy-four years later, three of them would have been identified as being someone else. The news that one of the Marines was not who everyone had thought he was all this time, came as a shock to the community; especially the families. The flag raisers were welcomed back as heroes, but they felt the real heroes were the ones that gave their life. As Ira Hayes said: "They were better men than me, and they're not coming back, much less back to the White House, like me."

One great help for the men on the front were war dogs. Several breeds were used, but Doberman-Pinschers were used most commonly. In total, some 10,000 dogs were trained during the war. Just like their human counterparts, dogs went through basic training and then received specialized training. They could be trained as messengers, and scouts, but were also used for sled pulling and mine detection.

Dogs and handlers were trained as teams. In fact, only the handler was allowed to feed, pet, or handle the dog. The dogs were taken on patrol during the day and night and gave a warning when they smelled an enemy soldier or a mine. They were trained to get used to heavy gunfire and were taught not to bark or growl, but to "freeze" at the smell or sound of danger.

When World War II ended, the war dogs were demilitarized. They were then offered to the families who had donated them. If they did not want them, the dogs were offered for sale.

We all know that war is not what we would wish upon any country. None of us wish conflict in everyday life, on the playground, or in politics. However, World War II was a time when several countries were in conflict. James L. Wheeler and Rene Gagnon Sr. were two of the many who answered the call. They were sent from California to meet up with their fellow patriots, collected from many states in our country. The young men said goodbye to their parents and loved ones. They had no comprehension how horrific this battle would be; they would live with the memories their entire lives, as most would have preferred to erase from their thoughts.

Rene Gagnon Sr. was one of those young patriots who felt the urgency to take the challenge and fight to protect his family, friends, and this great nation. At a young age, he joined the Marine Corps and left behind his mother, girlfriend, and a country that he would not let down. He found himself off to boot camp, from the East Coast to the West Coast to participate in training, to face the unknown. The glory of war set in motion a very romantic concept of American pride. Just like young Mr. Gagnon, he found himself on a naval carrier in the middle of the Pacific Ocean. Realizing they were destined to fight and possibly die on a remote island, quickly changed that self-esteem into a bitter challenge of reality.

Gagnon would soon have to face the devastating consequences of all that he was trained for. He was a radioman with the Fifth Marine Division and was instructed to become a runner. A now incomprehensible task, he was ordered to run a larger flag to the highest point of Mount Suribachi. He felt he was simply following command, never imagining his place in history.

Gagnon was there when the six Marines raised the second flag, and for decades he was believed to be one of the men who raised the flag. One would never have imagined the fame and attention. Soon after the picture was taken, he was cast into a position of being a national hero – one that he said he did not earn but should have been bestowed for the many casualties that had taken so many young lives. "Uncommon valor was a common virtue."

In October of 2019, extensive examination of footage revealed that it was in fact Corporal Harold "Pie" Keller who was the sixth man in the famous picture. Once again, one of the Marines had been misidentified. This news came as quite a shock to many.

During the battle, James L. Wheeler –who was proficient in math– was atop the volcano after a long and dangerous climb. He was a trained forward observer. Using optics, he would be able to spot enemy emplacements or movement from the high ground and relay the positions in coordinates to the mortar sections for indirect fire. A mortar was a three-man operated light mobile high angle artillery piece used by the ground units as they moved forward on enemy positions. After firing the first rounds, Wheeler would relay any adjustments critical to bring the mortar rounds on target until it was eliminated. Standing near him was Rene Gagnon Sr. They never knew each other, yet both were on the top of Mount Suribachi, fighting together. Even in such a terrible battle, simplistic things like recognizing another young man so many years after the fighting will forever be in a veteran's mind.

They fought one of the most terrible and bloodiest battles in American history. It was a war that was nothing like war today. They had very simple weapons compared to today, and little to nothing to protect themselves from enemy bullets.

The Marines had accomplished their mission, and the few remaining Japanese were cleared by the Army's 147th Regiment, that was brought in to relieve the departing battle-weary Marines.

The battle for Iwo Jima was the only battle in the entire war in which American casualties exceeded the Japanese. In just over a month of fighting, 27 Medals of Honor were awarded; one-third of the total number awarded during WWII. Close to 6,000 Americans lost their lives and only 216 of the 22,000 Japanese defenders surrendered.

It has now been nearly seventy-five years this battle. Many of our dads have passed away. We miss them and think of this battle which is often referred to as the bloodiest battle in history. They had to fight at such a young age. Those who survived would not talk about it for many years. They were humble men throughout their lives. They felt lingering thoughts and emotional scars forever, leaving many of their brother Marines behind, who were killed on the island. Marines believe something very special. They believe that once you have trained with a group of other young boys, to be Marines together, and you then fight side-by-side, you are truly brothers – even if you are not related by family.

At the end of the battle, the Marines were very careful to bury their fallen men with honor and tenderness. Almost three full divisions of Marines were on the tiny island, and each had a cemetery of their own so that their comrades could be buried properly.

So many years later, that flag and that photo still represent all the fighting Marines who did not make it home. They knew there was a chance that they wouldn't because they were joining the roughest and toughest branch of them all. One of the mottos the Marines have to this day is "First to fight." This is still very true, and it especially was during World War II.

Presently, the flag-raising photo represents people who believe in freedom. That remains a constant struggle in the world, truly good versus evil still now, even if the enemy is different. There will always be brave young boys –and now brave young girls– who are willing to fight so that freedom can be preserved. For the young Marines of today, the six flag raisers and all who fought in World War II are role models. We believe the Marines are more worthy of our respect and honor than athletes or famous people. They gave of their young days so that we could live ours. Of the boys who died it is often said that "they gave up their tomorrows so we could live our todays in peace."

On the Marine Corps Memorial, there is a quote from one of the navy commanders that defines all who fought at Iwo Jima. It says: "uncommon valor [another word for bravery] was a common virtue." Each one of those boys had the virtue of valor in his spirit, not to kill as many enemies as he could, but to protect as many brother Marines as he could. We will always remember the Marines of Iwo Jima for this one very precious value they upheld so well. This is one of the many reasons that the Marines' main motto is "Semper Fidelis." It is Latin and it means "Always faithful." They never give up, they never leave their brothers behind to die alone, and they fight to win.

Mr. Rosenthal's photograph and Felix De Weldon's monument –showcased in various construction through the world– will always symbolize the battle for Iwo Jima; honoring all of the young boys who made the ultimate sacrifice, as well as those who made it off the island. Only three of the six Marines who raised the flag made it home, where they helped the war effort by selling war bonds. The other three were killed during the campaign. Many people wanted the survivors to open up about their experiences during the battle. The veterans just wanted to forget the horrific and sad memories of the battle. With this statue and Mr. Rosenthal's photo, we will always have a memory etched in our minds of the brave who fought for our freedom.

About the Authors

Rene Gagnon Jr.

Rene Jr. is currently retired, after many years in the Home Improvement field. His life has been inspired after living in the shadows of his dad's legacy. With his father's being in the iconic photograph of the flag raising on Iwo Jima, his family has had its share of exposure across this great country. His father always attended events, not so much for personal gain, but as to bring honor and remembrance for those who sacrificed their all for the country. A graduate of the University of Miami, Rene Jr. has always tried living in the ideals his father raised him by. He and his co-author, Suzanne, are both trying to bring awareness to the next generation of pride and commitment that their fathers fought so valiantly for the country. Rene Gagnon resides in Franklin, NH, with his wife Judy, surrounded by their children, Sarah, Heather, Rebecca and Joshua.

Suzanne D. Wheeler

Ms. Wheeler's career began at the Central Intelligence Agency in the Office of Public Affairs as a media spokeswoman. She "hit the ground running," a supervisor once said of Ms. Wheeler. She was employed at the Agency in the midst of news stories of historic proportion in her role. Serving in the government for five Directors of Central Intelligence, she responded to numerous press inquiries. She resigned to raise her three sons; then working for non-profits and her own PR firm where she regularly promoted her father and his Iwo Jima experiences within the community and media placements to share his story. The greatest generation and her father's duty inspired her to promote and bring awareness to those of that era fought for freedom. She has, with other legacy made certain the sacrifices of other children of Iwo Jima dads, remain at the forefront.

Our Dads

Rene Gagnon Sr.

Returning home from the war with his bride, Rene set to building his home on a five-acre plot of land that he had purchased. He returned to his job at the "Chicopee Mills", where he had worked prior to enlisting in the Marines. He had mentioned in passing that his dream was to try and seek a job with the airline industry. His construction project was slightly delayed when it was announced that he would be getting a cameo in the John Wayne movie," Sands of Iwo Jima". Returning from California, completing the construction of his home, and starting his own construction company, and that long-awaited phone call came... a job with Trans Texas Airlines. The door was open. Within a year, an offer with Northeast Airlines and ultimately Delta. From that point, an offer to buy a travel agency with his wife Pauline. They moved Jubilee Travel Service to their home in Hooksett, NH. He passed away at the early age of 54 in October of 1979.

James L. Wheeler

James L. Wheeler was a former CIA deputy director of finance who retired in 1990, then vice president at USATrex International, an intelligence contractor. He spent most of his Agency career in the Far East and France. He was involved in several of the agency's covert operations, including a mission in which he helped recover hundreds of "bailout" kits that had been buried during World War II across Germany to aide downed pilots. These kits were commonly filled with gold coins that would allow Allied crew members to "buy" their way back to safety. Mr. Wheeler was a native of San Gabriel, California, and a 1951 graduate of Loyola Marymount University in Los Angeles. He received a master's degree in the technology of management from American University in 1973. Later in his life, he spoke regularly about his Marine Corps service during World War II and his participation in the battle of Iwo Jima; providing oral histories for museums and documentaries. Mr. Wheeler was a Marine Corps forward observer on top of Mount Suribachi for the first 10 days of the invasion in February 1945. Iwo Jima was one of the fiercest battles of the Pacific and a turning point against the Japanese. While with the CIA, his honors included the CIA Intelligence Medal of Merit. Jim had many interests including gardening, growing tomatoes, and making his mother's chili sauce recipe. He was admired by whomever he met. He was a loving, dutiful husband to Pat. He met her on assignment with the Agency, in Paris. He had one child, a daughter and later in his life, his three grandsons: James, Matthew, and Scott. He loved them more than life. As a former athlete, he was their most popular and regular spectator at sports events, especially hockey. They filled a void he always felt. Forever grateful for the love and admiration they returned to their Papa. James Lewis Wheeler passed away at the age of eighty-six, two days before Thanksgiving, in 2012.

Peter Doornekamp (contributor and editor)

Peter Doornekamp became interested in the battle for Iwo Jima while researching a thesis on World War II in the Pacific. Although this work focused on several islands, the intensity and ferocity of the battle for Sulphur Island made an impression of Peter, and it was not long before he decided to further research the battle. After two years of research that involved interviewing veterans of the battle, Peter published his book *Onto the Black Shores of Hell - the Battle for Iwo Jima*. Through the 'Iwo Jima Veterans and Families group' on Facebook, he got in contact with Suzanne Wheeler and Rene Gagnon. Peter lives in Amersfoort, the Netherlands, with his wife. He is currently writing a book about the battle for Okinawa.

DEDICATION

This book is dedicated to our dads, their parents, wives, loved ones, friends and other family members. Our fathers were called to duty and had to leave to fight in this unfamiliar territory. All Iwo Jima Marines and military who served, particularly those who gave their lives and were left behind on Mount Suribachi and on the rest of Sulphur Island, remain in our thoughts. They have been immensely recognized throughout the years, for their service to the United States of America by protecting our freedom – showcasing their selfless acts during combat.

We, the children, grandchildren, and relatives of the veterans, are enamored by the veterans' powerful sacrifice for our country. The authors' mission in this book is to convey the significance of this prominent historic battle, as well as exemplifying the notoriety of the statue –while understanding the background of the monument– and renaming the flag raisers.

All veterans' children are quite sentimental as they reflect upon the demons their heroes lived with throughout their lives. The battle now resonates in our daily thoughts. Presently, these soldiers and commanders of the greatest generation are in their nineties or deceased. It is consistent with our observations, as family members, that most rarely spoke to their loved ones about the horrific battle; yet the terrible memories were always a distraction in their minds, and now ours as we watch videos that we often do not wish to see. The children of Iwo Jima veterans are uniquely bonded, as they are now connected.

Thank you to our historians, contributors, and editors, in particular, Peter Doornekamp, who resides in the Netherlands.

Suzanne D. Wheeler

Printed in the United States
By Bookmasters